KINGFISHER
READERS

level
5

Explorers

Chris Oxlade

KINGFISHER

KINGFISHER

First published 2013 by Kingfisher
an imprint of Macmillan Children's Books
20 New Wharf Road, London N1 9RR
Associated companies throughout the world
www.panmacmillan.com

Series editor: Polly Goodman
Literacy consultant: Hilary Horton

ISBN: 978-0-7534-3102-3
Copyright © Macmillan Publishers International Ltd 2013

9 8 7 6 5 4 3

3TR/0815/WKT/UG/105MA

A CIP catalogue record for this book is available from the British Library.

Printed in China

Picture credits
The Publisher would like to thank the following for permission to reproduce their material. Every care has been taken to trace copyright holders. However, if there have been unintentional omissions or failure to trace copyright holders, we apologize and will, if informed, endeavour to make corrections in any future edition. (t = top; b = bottom; c = centre; r = right; l = left):
Cover Kingfisher Archive (KF); Apollo Program/NASA; KF; Shutterstock (SS)/ Alex Staroseltsev; 2l Corbis/ Imaginechina; 2cl KF; 2c NASA; 2cr KF; 2r KF; 3l KF; 3cl KF; 3c Alamy/World History Archive; 3cr Corbis/ Tui De Roy; 3r KF; 4 KF; 5r Alamy/Tetra Images; 6l Corbis/Monalyn Gracia; 7 KF; 8t KF; 8b KF; 9 KF; 10 KF; 11t Corbis/Sakamoto Photo Research laboratory; 11b Corbis/Imaginechina; 12 KF; 13cr KF; 13br KF; 14 KF; 15t KF; 15b SS/Yuri Yavnik; 16cl SS/Uryadnikov Sergey; 16–17 KF; 17cr SS/Loule Schoeman; 18–19 KF; 19 KF; 20 Getty/Universal History Archive; 21cr KF; 21tr KF; 21b SS/Dolnikov Denys; 22–23 KF; 24 KF; 25t KF; 25bl Alamy/Mary Evans; 25br Alamy/Simon Grosset; 26–27 KF; 27b KF; 28–29 KF; 29t Alamy/ Classic Image; 30 KF; 31t Alamy/Mary Evans; 31b Alamy/Lebrecht Collection; 32 KF; 33t KF; 33b Alamy/ World History Archive; 34 KF; 35 KF; 36–37 KF; 36 KF; 37 KF; 38 Corbis/Bettmann; 39t Alamy/RGS; 39b Corbis/Tui De Roy; 40 KF; 41t Corbis/HO/Reuters; 42 Apollo Program/NASA; 43t Apollo Program/NASA; 43b Apollo Program/NASA; 44 Corbis/Stephen Frink/Science Faction; 45t KF; Apollo Program/NASA; 46l Corbis/Imaginechina; 46cl KF; 46c NASA; 46cr KF; 46r KF; 47l KF; 47cl KF; 47c Alamy/World History Archive; 47cr Corbis/Tui De Roy; 47r KF

Contents

Life dates
Throughout this book, you will see dates in brackets after an explorer's name. These tell you when they lived. For example, Marco Polo (1254–1324) means that Marco Polo was born in 1254 and died in 1324.

Great explorers

Have you heard of Marco Polo, Christopher Columbus, David Livingstone or Roald Amundsen? They were famous explorers, who travelled through deserts and rainforests, over mountains, and across huge oceans and frozen lands to explore new places. They discovered places they didn't know existed, or places that nobody had ever been before.

These explorers were often away from home for many years. They didn't have accurate maps, and they faced terrible weather, disease and hunger. Some explorers survived using their skills, or because they just refused to give up. Others died on their **expeditions**.

The explorers in this book travelled to find new lands and claim them for their countries. They went to draw new maps, and to find things to trade, such as precious spices and gold. Sometimes they just went to find adventure.

Finding their way
The first explorers found their way by looking at the position of the stars and the movement of the Sun. By the eighteenth century, European explorers were using **navigation** instruments such as the **octant**, **compass** and **telescope**.

Telescope

Octant

Compass

Explorers made maps of the lands and coasts they found. Gradually they mapped more and more of the world.

New discoveries

NORTH
AMERICA

*Atlantic
Ocean*

*Pacific
Ocean*

SOUTH
AMERICA

The explorers in
this book made major
discoveries about our
world. They found lands
that Europeans had
not seen before, and
over hundreds of years,
they mapped the world.

Unfortunately, the explorers
often harmed the lives of
local people they met on
their travels. They took their
land, stole their possessions
and accidentally passed on
diseases that killed them.

These maps show the
routes of the explorers
in this book.

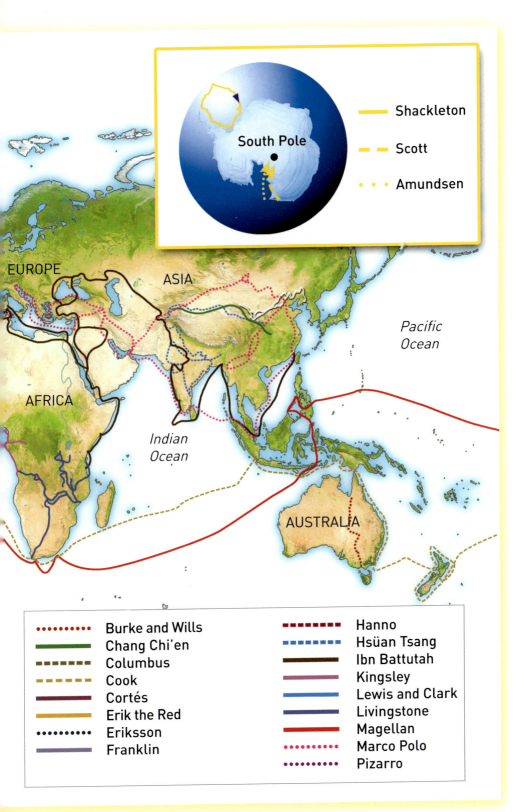

South Pole

Shackleton

Scott

Amundsen

EUROPE

ASIA

Pacific
Ocean

AFRICA

Indian
Ocean

AUSTRALIA

.... Burke and Wills

Chang Chi'en

Columbus

Cook

Cortés

Erik the Red

.... Eriksson

Franklin

Hanno

Hsüan Tsang

Ibn Battutah

Kingsley

Lewis and Clark

Livingstone

Magellan

.... Marco Polo

.... Pizarro

Explorers in ancient times

Some of the first explorers we know about were **Polynesian** people, who settled on islands in the Pacific Ocean about 3,500 years ago. They sailed across hundreds of kilometres of open ocean, from island to island, in big sailing canoes.

Polynesian boats had a platform in the middle to carry passengers and animals.

Chang Chi'en
The first-known Chinese explorer was called Chang Chi'en (200–114BCE). In 138BCE, he set off on a long journey West and travelled to great cities, including Rome. Chi'en was captured by a tribe called the Huns and imprisoned for ten years before he escaped.

More than 3,000 years ago, explorers from Egypt sailed up the River Nile, searching for precious goods such as gold, spices and perfumes to take back to Egypt.

More than 2,000 years ago, the Greeks, the Romans and the Phoenicians all explored the lands around the Mediterranean Sea. They went to find goods to buy and sell, and also to conquer new lands and build new cities.

The most famous Phoenician explorer was called Hanno. In 470BCE he sailed from the port of Carthage, in North Africa, down the coast of West Africa.

The Phoenicians traded goods such as cedar wood, dyed cloth, glass and wine, for materials such as ivory and silk.

Hsüan Tsang in India

Hsüan Tsang (602–664CE) was a **Buddhist** monk from China. Buddhism is a religion that was founded in India about 2,500 years ago. When he was 27 years old, Tsang made a **pilgrimage** to India, to learn more about Buddhism.

It was a long and dangerous journey of around 3,000 kilometres, over mountains and across deserts. Crossing one desert, he ran out of water and went thirsty for five days. When he finally reached India, Hsüan Tsang visited many Buddhist monasteries and collected religious **manuscripts**.

In the Bamiyan Valley, in modern-day Afghanistan, Hsüan Tsang was amazed by an enormous glittering statue of the Buddha, 53 metres high. He said: 'Its precious ornaments dazzle the eyes.'

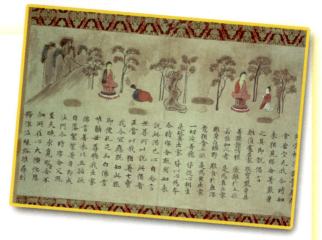

Hsüan Tsang translated manuscripts from India, written in a language called Sanskrit, into Chinese manuscripts like this one, the Inga Sutra.

Hsüan Tsang returned to China 16 years after he had left. He arrived home with many horses carrying hundreds of manuscripts and religious objects that he had collected on his travels. He spent the rest of his life translating the manuscripts into Chinese and writing down the story of his amazing journey.

An endless desert

On his journey to India, Tsang had to cross the Takla Makan Desert in the west of China, one of the biggest and sandiest deserts in the world. He would have had to survive hot, windy **sandstorms**. Even today, the only animals that can cross the desert and survive are camels.

Viking voyages

The Vikings lived in Scandinavia more than 1,000 years ago. They were expert ship-builders and sailors. They sailed to Britain, France, Spain and Russia to find new places to live and to **plunder** treasure. They also ventured out into the stormy Atlantic Ocean, where they discovered Iceland.

Viking ships were very sturdy, with space on deck for carrying goods and livestock, which the Vikings took to new lands where they settled.

Erik the Red was a famous Viking explorer. In 982CE Erik sailed from Iceland with his family, landed in the south of Greenland, and stayed there for three years. Erik sailed back to Iceland, then returned to Greenland with hundreds of settlers.

In about 1000CE, Leif Eriksson, one of Erik's sons, sailed from Iceland to North America. He landed on the island of Newfoundland. He was probably the first European to land in North America.

Leif Eriksson lands in North America after crossing the Atlantic Ocean.

Sun compass
Viking sailors might have used a wooden dial like this, called a sun compass, to check the direction in which to sail. Most of the time, Vikings stayed in sight of the coast and went ashore at night.

Marco Polo in China

Marco Polo (1254–1324) was born in Venice, in modern-day Italy. In 1271, when he was just 17 years old, he set off to China with his father and his uncle. They took gifts for **Kublai Khan**, the ruler of China.

Marco Polo crossed high mountains in Afghanistan on his way to China.

We don't know the exact route that Marco Polo took, but in Asia he followed an old trading route called the **Silk Road**. In 1275, four years after setting off, he arrived at the court of Kublai Khan.

The Polos at the palace of Kublai Khan.

Kublai Khan sent Marco Polo to different parts of his huge empire, to bring back information about the people who lived there. Marco was Kublai Khan's spy.

Marco Polo stayed in China for 17 years before returning home to Venice in 1295. He had been away for so long that his family and friends thought he was dead, so they were amazed to see him.

Amazing sights

In China, Marco Polo saw things he had never seen before, including kites and fireworks. He also saw paper money for the first time and wrote, 'With these pieces of paper they can buy anything.'

Marco Polo must have crossed the Great Wall of China on his travels. At the time, the wall was smaller and made of earth and stones.

Ibn Battutah

In 1325 a Muslim man called Ibn Battutah (1304–1369) left his home in Morocco. He was heading for Mecca, a holy city for Muslims, which is in modern-day Saudi Arabia. During the 5000-kilometre journey, Ibn Battutah grew to love travelling. So instead of going home from Mecca, he went exploring in what is now Iraq and Iran, and along the coast of Africa.

In Africa, Ibn Battutah saw hippos for the first time. He wrote that they looked like horses.

Ibn Battutah crossed the Sahara desert in a **caravan** of camels.

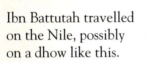

Ibn Battutah travelled on the Nile, possibly on a dhow like this.

Ibn Battutah then went to visit Sultan Muhammad of Delhi, one of the richest men in India, who asked him to take gifts to the Chinese ruler in Beijing. Ibn Battutah was amazed by the bustling Chinese cities he saw on his journey, but a war stopped him from reaching Beijing, and he decided that it was time to go home.

Columbus and America

Christopher Columbus (1451–1506) was a trader from Genoa (in modern-day Italy), who is famous for being the first European to discover America.

The king and queen of Spain wanted new **colonies**, so they paid Columbus to go on an expedition. Columbus was sure that if he sailed far enough into the Atlantic, he would reach Asia. He didn't know that America lay between Europe and Asia.

Columbus's three ships were the *Santa Maria* (the biggest), the *Niña* and the *Pinta*.

Columbus set out in 1492 with three small ships. They sailed for a month but didn't see any land. Finally, after 35 days at sea, they saw an island. Columbus thought he'd succeeded in getting to Asia. But he had actually found one of the islands that are now called the Bahamas.

Columbus went ashore in the Bahamas and claimed the new land for Spain.

Life at sea

Altogether there were about 90 men on Columbus' three little ships. Columbus had a small cabin, but the crew slept on deck, wherever they could find a space. They ate biscuits, dried meat and any fish they could catch.

Cortés and Pizarro

The lands that Christopher Columbus found in 1492 became known to Europeans as the New World, because they didn't know it had existed before. For Europeans, there was a whole new continent to explore. Dozens of European expeditions crossed the Atlantic to claim the land and find riches.

In 1519, Hernán Cortés (1485–1547), from Spain, went looking for a civilization of people called the Aztecs, who lived in modern-day Mexico. He marched through the jungle and found the Aztec capital city, called Tenochtitlan.

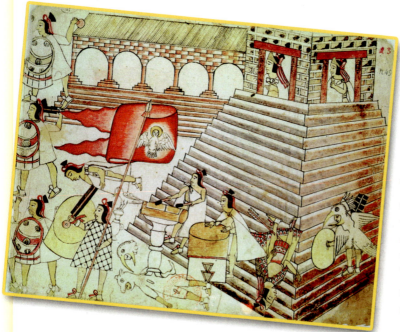

This picture shows Aztec warriors defending the temple of Tenochtitlan against Cortés and his men.

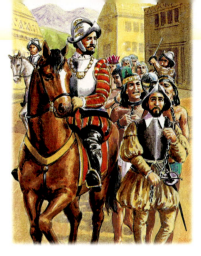

Hernán Cortés travelled with hundreds of armed soldiers.

Francisco Pizarro captured the Inca ruler, Atahualpa, and demanded gold as a ransom for his release.

Cortés and his men were amazed at the size of the city. They defeated the Aztecs in battle in 1521, destroyed the city, and took all the gold they could find back to Spain.

The promise of gold encouraged other Spanish explorers. Francisco Pizarro (1471–1541) ventured down the west coast of South America. He discovered the Inca civilization in Peru, conquered it and plundered its treasure.

Chocolate and tomatoes
The explorers who visited the Americas found plants that nobody in Europe had ever seen or tasted. They included cocoa (used to make chocolate), tomatoes, potatoes, sweetcorn, chilli peppers and peanuts.

Inca treasure

First around the world

Portuguese adventurer Ferdinand Magellan (1480–1521)
was the first explorer to sail around South America to
reach the Pacific Ocean. Magellan set off from Spain
in 1519, with five ships and 260 men. He sailed down to
the southern tip of South America and found a passage
through to the Pacific, now called the Strait of Magellan.

**Naming of
the Pacific**
When Magellan
sailed past South
America, he found an
ocean that was flat
and calm. He called
it the Pacific, which
means 'peaceful'.

Spain

NORTH
AMERICA

ATLANTIC
OCEAN

PACIFIC
OCEAN

SOUTH
AMERICA

The ships sailed
through the Strait
of Magellan.

One ship was
wrecked and
one returned
to Spain.

Magellan thought it would take a few days to cross the Pacific. It took months. Magellan's men ran out of fresh food, and many of them died from **malnutrition** and disease. Magellan threw his maps into the sea in despair, yet they still reached the Philippines.

In the Philippines, Magellan was killed in a fight with local people but one of his ships reached Spain in 1522. It was the first boat to sail all the way around the world.

ASIA

Magellan was killed, leaving two ships to continue the voyage.

AFRICA

Indonesia

Philippines

INDIAN OCEAN

PACIFIC OCEAN

AUSTRALIA

One ship was captured in Indonesia, leaving just one ship to sail back to Spain.

Cook in the Pacific

James Cook (1728–1779) was a captain in the British navy. In 1768, the British government sent Cook to search for a continent in the south of the Pacific. Cook sailed a long way south, but found nothing. He then sailed around New Zealand and Australia, drawing accurate maps of the coastlines.

Cook's party explored the east coast of Australia.

James Cook took scientists and artists on his expeditions, to record the landscapes, people, animals and plants they found.

On his next voyage he sailed as far south as he could before his ships were stopped by frozen seas. We now know this ice was surrounding the continent of Antarctica.

On his third voyage, Cook's men became the first Europeans to land on the islands of Hawaii, where Cook died in 1779. He was stabbed to death by locals in an argument over a stolen boat.

This is a modern replica of Cook's ship on his first voyage, the *Endeavour*.

Cook carried a very precise watch which allowed him to work out his exact **longitude**, and make accurate maps.

25

Lewis and Clark

In 1804, Meriwether Lewis (1774–1809) and William Clark (1770–1838) travelled all the way across North America to reach the Pacific Ocean.

The United States government wanted to survey the northwest of the United States, and find a route to the west coast of North America. They chose Lewis and Clark for the job. The two explorers set out from St Louis in May 1804, with 43 soldiers. Over the summer they paddled up the Missouri river in canoes, then built a log cabin to stay in over the winter.

Seeing the sea
When William Clark saw the Pacific Ocean in 1805, he said 'Great joy in the camp. We are in view of the ocean.'

Lewis and Clark canoed along rivers because it was faster than going over land.

They set off again in the spring. The hardest part was of their expedition was finding a way through the Rocky Mountains. A **native American** girl, Sacajawea, who knew some mountain passes, helped them. They eventually reached the Pacific Ocean in the autumn of 1805.

Lewis and Clark, with Sacajawea, reach the Great Falls on the Missouri river.

The Northwest Passage

About 500 years ago, explorers began searching for the Northwest Passage – a sea route around the north of America. Travelling here is difficult and dangerous. The sea is frozen all winter and there is a maze of islands to navigate through.

In 1845, Englishman John Franklin (1786–1847) set off with two ships, HMS *Erebus* and HMS *Terror*, and 128 men, to find the Northwest Passage. Two years later they hadn't come back, so a search party was sent. The rescuers found Franklin's ships stuck in the ice. The crews had run out of food, and Franklin had died in 1847. His men had tried to walk south to safety, but had all died too.

Amundsen finds a way

It was Norwegian explorer Roald Amundsen (see page 34) who finally found the Northwest Passage. Between 1903 and 1906 he sailed along it in a small boat with just six men and six dogs.

Franklin's last message

In 1859, a search party found a note buried in a pile of stones on King William Island, in the Northwest Passage. The note was written by Franklin's men, and reported Franklin's death in 1847.

Franklin's goggles were found by the search party in an abandoned boat.

Franklin and his crew had to abandon their ships in the Arctic wastes. With their ships gone, they had little chance of survival.

Mary Kingsley in Africa

When she was a little girl, Mary Kingsley (1862–1900) loved reading books about Africa. When her parents died, she decided to go to see Africa for herself. She wanted to meet the African people, study the plants and animals, and find adventure.

Kingsley didn't have any special clothes for exploring. Instead, she wore what most English women wore at the time: a long skirt and a blouse with a high neck. She always carried an umbrella, and took fish hooks, tobacco and cloth to trade for food and other things she needed. She travelled with help from local people.

Saved by a skirt
In 1895 Mary Kingsley fell into an animal trap. Her thick skirt saved her from being injured by the sharp spikes at the bottom of the pit!

Mary Kingsley exploring along the Ogowe river in Gabon, in about 1895.

On her travels, Kingsley collected fish from African rivers for the British Museum, some of which were named after her.

The Water Babies

Mary's father, Charles Kingsley, wrote a famous book called *The Water Babies*, about a boy who goes on adventures around the world. Mary must have read it. She couldn't wait to go on her own adventures.

Livingstone in Africa

Many explorers from Europe went to Africa in the nineteenth century. David Livingstone (1813–1873) was one of the most famous. Livingstone travelled to Africa in 1840 to be a **missionary**. He set up two missions in the south of Africa, but he found that he enjoyed exploring more than missionary work.

Livingstone's first taste of exploration was in 1849, when he crossed the Kalahari desert. In 1855 he travelled down the great Zambezi river and discovered the towering Victoria Falls.

Livingstone was the first European to look over the Victoria Falls, on the Zambezi river. He named them after the British queen.

David Livingstone meets Henry Morton Stanley in Africa, in 1871.

In 1866, Livingstone began hunting for the source of the River Nile. Nobody heard from him for years, and search parties were sent to look for him. Henry Morton Stanley, a reporter for the *New York Herald* newspaper, finally found him in 1871, but he couldn't persuade Livingstone to leave Africa with him. Livingstone died from malaria, a tropical disease spread by mosquitoes, in 1873.

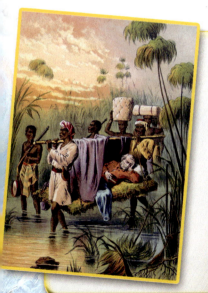

Livingstone's last expedition
Livingstone became ill during his search for the source of the Nile, and his helpers carried him through the swamps. When he died, two helpers took his body 1,600 kilometres to the coast.

Across Australia

Australians Robert O'Hara Burke (1821–1861) and William John Wills (1834–1861) led the first expedition to cross the continent of Australia from south to north. Burke and Wills set off from Melbourne in 1860, with 19 men. They set up a camp at a place called Cooper Creek. Then Burke, Wills, John King and Charlie Grey continued northwards.

The four men struggled through thick forests and baking deserts. After 57 days they reached the north coast of Australia. They turned back for home, but hunger, bad weather and illness slowed them down, and Grey died. They finally staggered back to Cooper Creek, but the other members of the expedition had gone. Burke and Wills died at Cooper Creek. John King lived with a group of **Aboriginal people** until he was rescued months later.

Camel transport

Burke and Wills left Melbourne with two years' worth of supplies, 23 horses, six wagons and 26 camels. The camels were brought from India, and chosen because they could survive in hot deserts.

Burke, Wills and King were exhausted and sick when they got back to Cooper Creek.

Amundsen in the Antarctic

Roald Amundsen (1872–1928) was a Norwegian explorer. He led the first expedition ever to reach the South Pole.

In 1910, Amundsen sailed to Antarctica on his sturdy ship, the *Fram*. He set off from his base on the coast of Antarctica in October 1911, at the start of the summer. He took four sledges, pulled by teams of dogs.

Amundsen's ship, the *Fram*, was built to stand up to the thick **pack ice**.

Local skills

Between 1905 and 1908, Amundsen lived and travelled in the Arctic. He learned many skills from the local Inuit people, such as making clothes from furs and driving teams of sledge dogs. These skills helped him to reach the South Pole.

Amundsen planted a Norwegian flag at the South Pole and then turned back for home.

Amundsen and his men struggled for weeks, over mountains and glaciers. He finally reached the South Pole on 14 December 1911. British explorer Robert Falcon Scott got there just 34 days later. (See page 38 for more about Scott.)

Dog teams pulled Amundsen across the ice and snow.

Scott and Shackleton

In 1911–1912, British explorer Robert Falcon Scott (1868–1912) and four other men walked 1,300 kilometres to the South Pole, only to find that Roald Amundsen had beaten them to it. On the way back, the men slowly ran out of food. Two men died from exhaustion and **frostbite**. Scott and the other two struggled on, but were trapped in their tent by a storm, where they died. They were just 18 kilometres from a food store, where they would have been safe.

Scott and his team pose for a photograph with Amundsen's Norwegian flag.

Antarctic food
Pemmican was a high-energy food that Scott and Amundsen both took for their sledging trips. It was made with dried meat and fat, and was often used to make a stew called 'hoosh'.

Shackleton's men launching the *James Caird*, in which
Shackleton sailed to the island of South Georgia to get help.

In 1915, the ship of another British Antarctic explorer,
Ernest Shackleton (1874–1922) was crushed by sea ice.
Shackleton and his men then drifted on **ice floes** for
five months before using boats salvaged from the ship to
escape to an island. Then Shackleton and a few others
sailed 1,300 kilometres across the ocean to get help.
All his men were saved.

An ice floe near
Elephant Island,
Antarctica, where
Shackleton's men
survived for four
months while
Shackleton
fetched help.

Norgay and Hillary

Tensing Norgay (1914–1986) and Edmund Hillary (1919–2008) were the first explorers to climb to the summit of Mount Everest, the highest mountain in the world. Mount Everest is in the Himalayas. It is called Chomolungma by local people, which means 'Holy Mother'. It is 8,848 metres high.

Tensing and Hillary on Everest's summit

Oxygen equipment

High on Everest, the air is very thin, which makes it hard to breathe, especially when doing exercise such as climbing. Tensing and Hillary took oxygen in bottles, which they breathed through masks.

Edmund Hillary (left) and Tensing Norgay (right) after descending safely from the summit

Tensing Norgay was a local man called a sherpa. He was an expert mountaineer, and helped to carry equipment up the mountain. Edmund Hillary was from New Zealand. They were part of a large expedition, and were chosen to make an attempt on the summit. They reached their goal at 11.30 in the morning, on 29 May 1953. They had succeeded where many climbers had failed before, and they soon became world famous.

Summit
Route
Everest

The route that Tensing and Hillary took to the summit of Mount Everest.

Armstrong on the Moon

American astronaut Neil Armstrong (born 1930) was the first person to stand on the surface of another world – the Moon. Armstrong was commander of the *Apollo 11* spacecraft, which flew to the Moon in 1969. The other crew members were Edwin 'Buzz' Aldrin and Michael Collins.

It took two days to travel to the Moon. Collins stayed in the **command module**, while Armstrong and Aldrin descended to the Moon's surface in the **lunar module**. Their fuel supply got dangerously low as they searched for a place to land, but Armstrong stayed calm and got down safely. A few hours later, wearing a spacesuit, Armstrong stepped carefully on to the Moon's dusty surface.

Apollo 11 was launched into space by a giant Saturn V rocket.

On the surface

When Armstrong stepped on to the Moon, he said the now-famous words 'That's one small step for man, one giant leap for mankind.' Back on Earth there was great excitement about the Moon landings. Around 500 million people were watching as Armstrong took his historic steps.

Armstrong and Aldrin set up experiments, took photographs, and collected rocks to take back to Earth.

The astronauts clambered down a ladder on to the Moon's surface.

Modern exploration

There are still many undiscovered places in the world. On the Yucatán Peninsula, in Mexico, there are huge networks of underwater caves. These cave networks are like mazes, and divers have to be careful not to get lost. In these caves, scientists have discovered types of animals found nowhere else on the planet.

These divers are exploring amazing underwater caverns on the Yucatán Peninsula, in Mexico.

The ocean floor is another place that people have hardly explored. Some parts are thousands of metres underwater, which is too deep for most submarines to reach.

In March 2012, the **submersible** *Deepsea Challenger* reached the bottom of the Challenger Deep, nearly 11 kilometres under the Pacific Ocean. The pilot was film director James Cameron, who spent three hours exploring the ocean floor before returning to the surface.

Robot submersibles have allowed us to explore the deep ocean landscape and the creatures that live there.

Space exploration

The Moon is the furthest that human explorers have reached into space. In the future, astronauts may visit Mars. Until then, robot **space probes** such as *Opportunity*, which landed on Mars in 2004, are exploring the amazing solar system for us.

Glossary

Aboriginal people The Australian Aboriginal people are the original inhabitants of Australia.

BCE Before the Common Era (any date before 1CE).

Buddhist A person who follows Buddhism (a religion founded by the Buddha).

caravan A group of traders or pilgrims travelling across a desert.

CE The Common Era (any date after 1CE).

colony An area of land where people from another country settle, live and trade, and are controlled by the other country.

command module The section of spacecraft that the astronauts left and returned to Earth in.

compass A navigation instrument with a magnetic needle that always points North.

expedition A journey that is taken for a special purpose, such as to explore a place.

frostbite Damage, normally to fingers, toes and the nose, caused by exposure to extremely cold temperatures.

ice floe A large sheet of floating sea ice.

Kublai Khan A very powerful ruler of China, who lived in the 13th century CE.

longitude An imaginary line around the Earth, from the North to the South Pole, which is used to measure distances.

lunar module The section of spacecraft that took astronauts between the command module and the Moon's surface.

malnutrition A lack of proper nutrition, caused by not eating enough food, or having an unhealthy diet.

manuscript A book or other document, written by hand.

missionary A person on a mission to try to spread their religion.

native American An original inhabitant of Canada and the USA.

navigation Planning the course of a journey and finding the way.

octant A navigation instrument used to measure the height of stars from a moving ship.

pack ice Large pieces of sea ice that have been squeezed together.

pilgrimage A journey to a place that is sacred to a religion, such as Mecca for Muslims.

plunder To steal using force.

Polynesian A person from an area of the Pacific Ocean that includes Hawaii, Samoa and the Cook Islands.

sandstorm A strong wind carrying clouds of sand and dust.

Silk Road An ancient trading route between China and eastern Europe, named after the silk that was transported along the route.

space probe A robot spacecraft sent to another planet, or moon, to take photographs and collect scientific information.

submersible A small submarine used for scientific research or underwater exploration that can work in waters that are too deep for divers.

telescope A navigation instrument used to make objects appear nearer.

Index